A TOUCH OF LOVE

Hugh Williams

First published in 2000 by
Cromwell Publishers
Eagle Court Concord Business Park
Threapwood Road
Manchester M22 0RR

Paperback ISBN 1-901679-62-4

iii

The first of these poems, 'How far the clouded sky' was written during a rather boring meeting in Newcastle a number of years ago. Most of the others followed at intervals in fairly quick succession, but a few are of much later date. However romantic they may appear to be, the early ones were written during a difficult time. As to whom they are addressed, I have no comment to make.

They are, of course, dedicated to Stephanie, my wife.

Who?

Who spoke,
Who called to me,
Who whispered in the darkness of the night?

Who knew,
Who read my mind,
Who guessed at secrets hidden from their sight?

Who came,
Who touched my heart,
Who showed me unimagined heights above?

Who look'd,
Who gave thy name,
Whose beauty illumined the paths of love?

Love At First Sight

It was late that day,
That late December day,
When we first met.
The blacked-out street
Was silent, wet
And dense.
To our heightened sense
Very life seemed fleet.

Between our clasped hands
Happiness hung
Upon a thread
Of blood
That ran
Bright red
And gently swung
Betwixt.
We kissed, a soft
Mucosal kiss,
Our breath mingled,
Rose and vanished
In the mist.

We had no speech
But with our eyes
And each to each
Love flowed
Took flame and glowed.
We gazed and smiled
And laughed with joy
And walked on
In the dark.

Now, fifty years away
I know what love is,
First tasted then,
That late December day.

The Seeker

Oft have I dreamed upon this waiting hour.
Within my hand a pen, poised as to write.
Within my breast the burning passion fire
That streams itself, in turning anxious flight.

Oh come, fair muse, inspire dull-witted brain
To act it's part as agent of the soul,
And speak with liquid tongues of scorching flame
From that fierce furnace of the heart below.

The Kindling Spark

Since that very day when first you came,
So young, so innocent,
Into this barren plot I thought existence;
And took this withered heart
And breathed it with new life,
That I might see again
Through doors long barred, and clouded window pane,
Beyond the dark horizons where
The wheeling flights of loaded vultures stare;
Beyond the imperspicuous murk
And foaming ocean's swell,
To fairer, brighter lands, where dwell
Those 'happy few' who are no longer bound
By fleshly ties to this devouring ground,
Who in their genius crowd the voiceless air,
Now filled with song.

This have I seen,
And now
The simple mention of your name
Is as a kindling spark,
And from the dark vaults of my mind
Come tumbling words, and sounds defined
That I can hear;
And in the racing circuits of the brain
Melodic themes now rise and fall again,
And with their surcease, and for a space,
A certain peace endures.

How Far The Clouded Sky

How far the clouded sky,
How high the mountains climb,
How clear my own heart's cry
For love I hoped was mine.

The furthest distance run,
The widest space made near,
The longed-for time now come
For all I held most dear.

But can this all be so?
Can life fulfil its dream?
Can this late time to know
Enhance the sunset gleam?

I know the time is short,
I know the pall is nigh
I know there is no fault,
To love is not to die.

You have my heart in thrall,
You may do what you will,
You can raise up, let fall,
Love shall be with you still.

If It Be Love

If it be love that makes the spinning world
Incontinent upon its axis turn,
And in fair company of planets hurl
Concentric orbits of an aging sun.
If true affection breathes the warming wind
That wakes new life within a winter'd tree,
And shakes the daffodils of early spring,
While from the melting snows the streams run free.
If surging passion heaves the ocean's breast
And piles the storm-clouds in a castled sky,
Or drives the endless torrents without rest
And fills the scented air with silent cry.
Then would you be the world, the wind, the sea,
The sky, the storms, the lighted spring to me.

The Awakening

There's an awakening
Beside ruffled water,
A stirring on the hills,
A swelling of bright rills,
A rush of birds,
And eyes
Lifted to light skies
Pale blue
Above the snow,
Reflect the racing clouds.
On shadow'd rocks, below
The serene towers
You sit
Beside the pelting beck,
And silence lies about you.

Or on the farthest peak
Some prehistoric gods look down
Benevolent,
To kiss your beauty with the sun.
Night's hours come,
And e'en the ancient stars,
Cast in unimagined space,
Brave the icy dark
And bow to your delight.

Untenant Heart

Now have I travelled wide the spans of earth,
And crossed in ships the vast foam-crested seas.
I've flown above the lands of ancient birth,
And seen a thousand suns rise in the east
To light the golden tips of minarets,
And set the purple mountains into flame
With all prodigious Nature's glories. Yet
There is no beauty, but with which thy claim
Has no dispute in this untenant heart.
I may not taste where sucks the honey bee,
Nor with a kiss it's nectar do impart,
Nor where the startled faun runs may I flee,
But certain know wherein thy sweetness lies,
In voice, and touch, and in thy loving eyes.

The Quiet River

On Summer evenings, when tall shadows lie
Prostrate across the golden sward,
Cast in the fairest mould of trees and spires
Immobile, save to mark the swinging earth
Intent upon its axial vertigo.
Above, high buttressed walls, austere and vast
In solemn grey, burned by the sinking light
To saffron and old rose;
While from each cornice featured gargoyles peer
Down huge arched windows, delicately traced,
Dark-faced in their repose;
And, crowning all, immensity of towers
Reeling against bright clouds,
Three straining fingers, reaching up to God.

So in such peaceful company do I
Alone upon the graceful lawns keep pace
With my imprisoned thoughts, in such impasse
They beat upon my brain to seek release,
And failing, take respite in dreams, to flee
The cornered confines of reality.
So then I see
Myself,
Not lonely now, but hand in hand with thee
And heart in heart.
Ah, love, would'st thou could be
So true!
Wandering once more the beaten paths
Among strange woods and unfamiliar hills,
Past unknown landmarks, through the purple baths
Of twilight,
Into the star-shot umbra of the night.
And resting on the river's honeyed banks
Watch an ancient moon lift beyond the sills

Of Heaven,
To dance reflection on the water's flow,
Shimmering as the fireflies might, and go
Climbing the archèd crescent of the sky
To reach it's zenith.
Silent there we lay
Unmoving, nor a single word to say
Reshaped our lips, that clung each upon each
With mingled breath, and twinéd hands that spoke
The promises our hearts could not revoke.
There, beneath th'ethereal queen's wan blush,
Was pledged and sealed the bond, in that first flush
Of ecstasy, beside the quiet river.
And thou, the giver,
Generous of thy gifts
That steeped mine eyes in beauty, all thine own,
And like a mirror held before the sun,
Woke within my heart another dawn,
Of such bright day
That stripped the darkest shadow from my mind.
So we went on, and saw night creatures play
Among the hedgerows and the open fields,
And heard pale fishes rising in the stream,
Caught the faint sweet scent where roses grow
Climbing old garden walls; reflected gleam
Of eyes unblinking, secretive,
That vanished without trace.
And in dark space,
And silently, my joyous spirit, thinking
Here I belong.

If I Touch Your Hand

There's scent of springtime blossom in your hair,
Full summer green
Lies deep as limpid pools within your eyes.
Upon your lips a generous surprise,
And with the twain
There's honey in your mouth
And soft sweet breath,
Echoes dreams of South,
Caress my cheek.

Then, if I touch your hand,
Thus
And thus, in that rich land
Held within your palm,
My heart rests quiet, calm
In the timeless joy, at your command.

The Truth

Your presence in my heart is like the sun
That pours in through some gloomy casement pane,
To shine about an old forgotten room
Full of dust and secrets, and the shame
Of bitter words once uttered, long ago
That hang in stale air, as a miasma
Drifts across a stagnant pool.

Your love within my heart is as the wind
That sweeps across the scented moors and sea,
Bearing in the clear and mounting air
The happy cries of birds,
Which, entering the shadow'd chambers, wafts
The sickly mist aside, that I now see
The truth you show to me.

A Crowded Place

Let love not speak in words, but with a chance
Encounter of young hands,
A glance across a crowded place,
A light within a smiling face,
And then, the heated city streets
Are paved with golden sands
Stretched to a summer sea,
And distant lands
Familiar with loving tones
That speak your name.
O Love, your pain
Is sweetness of a kiss
As honey in my mouth.
Unspoken words
Imprint upon my lips
And in my hand a sword,
Unsheathed, to guard
The honour of your gift.

Song Unsung

How bright the candle burns, and still the flame
That, steady in the breathless dark, gives light
To shadows, and the silence of the night
That lies without the clamour of my brain.
To still the frantic mind's mad roundabout,
The storm and discord, panic and dispute,
Now school my thoughts to quell the rising shout
And live with you, where beauty's attribute
Lies in your heart, and pray to feel your hands,
Light as dawn's breeze, lay down my harsh felt tone;
And, holding mine, across the drifting sands
To wander, harmonious and alone.
A breathless song lies waiting on my tongue
But dumb hand writes the melody, unsung.

I Met You

Cold, and on the lonely road
That leads to nowhere,
I met you.
A row of shuttered houses
And streaming cobbles underfoot.
In the valley
A thousand chimneys lift against the light,
All are dead, and
The silent city empty.
The dark wind blows,
There's not a word to read
In nameless streets.

Beaten, in the heat of wilderness
I met you.
In an arid landscape
Burning grey
That never knew before the touch of man
Or any living thing.

I heard you say
"You are alone"
I nodded, silently
And with no other word you took my hand
And from that fearsome lonely land of mine
You led me.

There is no other time that I have lived
But since I knew I had your precious gift
Of love.

The Hope

How can I speak of love,
Whose very words are favours,
To my love?
My heart is overflowing,
To be the very essence of a man,
I cannot then conceal from you the hope
That all men live for, that within your arms
I find my consummation, and the dream
That all men dream of, realised.
Yet, I seek no pleasure, save your own.
Waiting, and waited on, the very one
And sister to my one that lies within
Can I then ask of you that blessed hand
To rest upon my own, caress my lips
With yours, and from a burning eye pluck tears
Born of the welling flood about my heart.

Doubts

I caught a passing glimpse of you today,
A single searing glance.
Did you, I wonder, see me? Did you say
"It was the merest chance."
Perhaps;
But with one stroke,
Like the enchanting sorcerers of old,
Whose spells set fire to weaker hearts and cold
Than mine,
Your beauty fanned the embers into flame,
And once again
Am I in that dark limbo of delight
Where all is sweet surmise,
And nothing certain lies
But in your heart.
Ah! would you not be part
Of mine?
Or in fair time
Resolve me of such doubts

That cloud my mind.
For if you do not speak
Then am I left
To answer my own heart,
And being weak
Fall prey to those illusions passion brings.
So thus I think:
"It is her shyness that does hold her tongue
And though she would, she may not, for such sake,
Speak her whole mind, but secretly does take
This offer".
Or, in some pensive mood:
"She is averse, but seeks not to offend,
If no word spoke, no injury to mend".
And so betwixt these two extremities
Swings like a pendulum my toiling mind
Waking and sleeping.
Speak then.

The Wood

Listen!
I can hear the night birds call
The owls hoot
And nightingales in song
Down in the wood.
Come with me,
For the Summer's term is brief
And soon the nights are long
And dark, the birds have flown
To the far South,
And the nests are empty
Derelict and cold;
And standing in the wood
I am alone.
Be with me, then,
And hold my hand, and talk,
And when the pale sun rises
On another year, we'll walk
Together on the trodden path
And to the silent wood,
And waiting
Listen for the Wanderer's return
And I'll not be alone.
For there's another Summer,
Bright and clear,
Which has no winter'd end
Lying in Time's hand
Waiting.
And I am made the land
And you the sun.
When that time comes,
And this cold earth is warmed
And nourished by your beauty
There'll be no snow,

Nor will the North winds blow.
A few brief Summer rains
That will enhance your glow
And be my gains
Of understanding.
Love, I know,
Gleams in the sunbeam's light
And in the whispers
Of a Summer's night
And in the breeze
That stirs the Summer leaves
Love speaks
Down in the wood.

The Radiant Stars

The radiant stars
Stand vigil while you sleep,
And in their paths
The circling planets keep
Account of years.

Take your repose
With easy heart and clear,
The long day's close,
Unhindered by vain fears,
Of welcome night.

And, when you wake,
Let no false dawn deceive
The true daybreak,
With morning scents to breathe
From dew-deck'd grass.

Then sweet the light
That lies within your eyes
Captive delight
Of high bright summer skies.

The Arrow

Across the sky in masses dark and slow
The solemn clouds in bleak procession go
Over the landscape in white-mantled snow,
While constant arctic northern winds do blow.

So if my heart be broken, let it be
In Winter, when the days are short and grey,
And nights are long and bitter cold to me,
When my true love's to sunny climes away.

I knew you, spoke to you, gazed in your eyes,
Saw Summer sunshine glinting in your hair,
Knew all your loveliness in each disguise,
In sheepskin wrapped against inclement air.

I've seen you scarved against autumnal rain
And in the daily froing take your part
And if I love you, am I then to blame?
For who can tell which arrows pierce the heart.

The Song

In knowledge of thee, I have touched the heights,
Walked the crests of mountains,
Breathed the heady air of ecstasy,
Spoken with gods, and heard the song of life
Clear and true, a single sounding note
Arcing up, beyond ethereal blue
To the very vault of Heaven.
O, I have paced the loneliness of heather
Soft in the summer light,
And listened to the mesmerising bees
Intent upon their search.
Now heard the clatter of an eagle's wings
Among foreboding crags,
Watched the Imperial soaring in the sky,
To swoop upon the beast that tardy lags
Beyond its sanctuary.
I have plunged my hands into the stream
Virginal from the moor,
And waded barefoot on the dancing pebbles,
And sat along the steamy rolling banks
The while the night mist rises as a dream
To dim the shining brilliance of the Moon.
I knew the song within me then conceived,
But to thine honour born,
To sense the flow of thoughts articulate
As free as springtime rain upon the air.
The key thy gentle hand has turned
Unlocked the secret door I could not find.
From there this spirit to high pastures climbed
To seek the healing wind.

Minds

A meeting of two minds,
A fleeting touch,
A brief contract
Unsealed and yet unsigned,
And out of such
Burns a single instant
A flame of love.

A greeting of two hearts
In passing met.
A swift caress
From each to each imparts
A joy, but yet
It is a sweet regret
To say farewell.

The Citadel

I never spoke to thee of love,
I never held thy hand
Nor kissed those cherished lips,
Nor touched thy hair, that sits
Crown-like about thy face.
But in the secret place
Within my breast,
There thou did'st reach my heart
That beats in such unrest;
Lay gentle siege
And take the citadel.
Unknown, by soft intrigue,
Unheralded, it fell,
And silently. Thy spell,
Cast in fair disguise
Of beauty, and surprise
In mine own weakness, yield
I this wanton field
To thee.

My blood runs red
Across the summer green,
And myriad streams
Now in thine honour stained
Imperial purple,
Mingling, by rivers drained
To flow toward the sea.

The Face

I saw a place where beauty glows
Enlivened by the rich blood flows
Beneath that skin, so soft and fair
'Tis like a blossom shining there.

And from the skeleton of bone,
By exquisite artistry done,
The gentle contours integrate
And make perfection's intimate.

Above, the high-arched brows reflect
The smiling lips sweet upward lift
Revealing serried tips of pearl
Gleaming like some precious jewels;
And level set, a grey-blue light
Shines softly in the orbs of sight.

So wide and cool, as marble ground
This forehead with the soft hair crown'd.
Do you not recognise that place
Sweet friend? It is your lovely face.

The Sleeping Tiger

Apart you stand, and silent, biting lip,
What mood is this, to furrow that sweet brow?
Or that dear heart, endow'd with generous gift
Enclosed, asleep, and gently drifting now
Among strange dreams, beyond the touch of man.
Would not this willing flesh of mine now turn
The golden key within the lock, and then
Pour out this coursing blood in hope new born
To wake the sleeping tiger. Blood in blood,
The crimson streams now mixed in passion flow,
And mounting levels pour in quiet flood
Through vast and empty caverns far below
The smooth exterior of conscious mind
To fill those dark recesses of the soul,
Seeking the peace that only love can find,
Beyond conceit of man, to make the whole.

Joy

Because of you
I am in spirit born again,
And feeling, dead
As dreams imaginéd,
With life restored, but not the same
As used to be.
Now joy is come once more to me
Because of you.

Witness

I would I were a Shakespeare, or a Keats,
To put my thoughts to lambent words;
Or like the Psalmist, sing my passions out.
Faint shadow can my voice afford
To such as these; poor mortal, in such doubt
To speak my mind and heart aloud,
And ring the changes on a single chord.

But come, take courage, sing your lonely song,
Break silence to declaim your art.
Such feeling should not be contained too long
Lest, turning on itself, your heart
Should rend itself, and then may sing no more,
And all be lost, which may be won,
And life itself becomes a life alone.

And so, sweet friend, bear witness to my love
For you, and match your heart to mine
If such may be; if not, your love's your own,
And so enjoy the two, whilst I,
Fortune entailed, can play the lovesick clown
Hoping vain hope, with simpered eye,
Or wear a smiling face, to hide the scar.

Beauty

Fair one, whose beauty no man can compare
Give kind regard to these imprudent words
That I should speak my heart where none should dare,
And foolishly rush in, by angels heard.

Speak not of love, but rather worshipped be
So far are you beyond my vainest thought.
Hide not yourself for mortal eyes to see
That privilege is paid and dearly bought.

That gracious Helen, whom the Greeks revered
And for her sake in ten long years of war
Lost many heroes, by the Trojans fear'd,
And Troy in ruin, that Aeneas saw;
Could not, in all her loveliness, behold
To you a micron in fair advantage;
But rather in your angel brilliance fold
And seek for consolation in dotage.

In the ill-starr'd love that Shakespeare wrote of,
Of Juliet whose beauty was acclaimed,
And held poor Romeo to fatal end,
And in their death two famous houses shamed.
This story is a wonder of the world
To illustrate the tragedy of love.

But were you living at that hour, unfurled
The flower of your loveliness above
Would outbloom Juliet, and Romeo
Perforce would give his name to other lines
And speak your name in passion, were not so
That you are here and I now know the times.

Think not in likeness Romeo of me,
Such gentle gallantry as his nature
In that great Poet's deathless words all see.
Comparison of that grace or fair feature,
It ill becomes me to aspire to such.
But I am what I am, and that is yours.
All that I am, and that much is that much.
'Tis so and may not be repeated more,
For now I have declared myself; in brief
I love you, and thus am part of love.

Love's Melodies

I am not gold, nor decked about with flowers
Perfumed as summer roses, and mine eyes
Do not, as would the sea,
Reflect the soaring blue of southern skies.
My tongue is not an instrument sweet tuned
To play love's melodies, nor speak too vain.
My heart is more than flesh and blood can hold
That lies within me, and I know what pain
Can do, yet do my hands enfold
Your own.

The Prize

Long had I wandered, lonely and bereft,
Amid the vales of sadness and despair,
And seen the many gloomy caverns there
Filled with the bitter seeds defeat has left.

Nor was there any break in lowering clouds
That I might glimpse the sun-kissed peaks afar,
Nor any signpost on the narrow road
That straight as arrow's flight o'ersteps the bar.

In that dark valley I could see no light
Until your hand took mine, and then my night
Began to pale, and through the drifting race,
Faintly at first, sunshine upon my face

And warm; and turning, look'd into your eyes
To see, in their reflection, my one prize.

Time

If time has any meaning, then it is
The time I breathe and hold you in my arms,
The time your hand takes mine
And intertwine.
The time I hear your voice,
The time I see your face.
All else is but the passage of a clock
Its idle hands in limbo, as they drift
Around the faceless feature, numberless
To me.
My time is in you, and before this day
I had no voice, no reason, no desire
For living.
In my mind
That liv'd upon the edge of consciousness,
Alive, I grant you, but as others live
That have no spirit.
Instinct guides their hope,
And without it hopeless must I be.
I say that in my mind lay many dreams
Damned by the dark reality that hung

Like aging clouds, reluctant to reveal
The secrets of the stars that lie beyond.
And I, no longer fearful but indifferent,
Held all in disregard, with love for none.
The passage of bleak years, but of no time,
Went all unheeded. Age sought to thicken
Arteries, and thin the coursing blood.
While I,
All unaware of their encroaching flood
Lived, timeless, day by day, steeped in deep sin
Lost in mine own despair.
I did not think of time, encircled thoughts
Wandered the mazes, seeking no release
From a dulled brain.
Only the pale flame,
A pin-point in my dreams, burn'd clear and true.
But from the well-spring of your generous heart
That opens like a rose beneath the sun,
Scented, wonderful, rich in rich things
Love in love's ardour to fruition brings.

Strangers

If you seek proof, look into my heart,
There find no lust upstart
To steal a night's release,
Nor think to gaze on peace
Or tranquil scenes.

Love's fire gleams
Blood-red, amid the arrows of his art,
And Passion's flame
Casts shadows, flickering as a thought
Across a vacant brain.

Nor is there joy, but yet
Within the void
A gaping pain,
No privilege enjoyed
The times we meet,
No smile to greet
Mine own.

And though I've known
Your face a thousand years
Your beauty blinds me still
In welcome tears.

How strange it be,
When no thing is the same,
That strangers we
Remain.

The Mood Of Love

Now through the desolate years of loneliness
Thy beauty, like a star, has guided me
As some frail ship, beset by fierce storms
In darkest northern sea,
Has for it's compass that fix'd Polar Star
That lends such faith to praying mariner
As I have had.
No need have I of doubt, for in my heart
Such sentiment as clears the dubious mind
And bids my head be ruled, not in part
Of reasoned logic, but with fire.
For reason says: Be wise,
Have care,
Withdraw while yet there is the chance;
Exclude your eyes from penetrating glance,
And close your ears
To sweetly sounding nuance,
An even tenor of a life to gain
To taste no joys, but feel no pangs of pain.
To this hearts make reply:
What travesty of life existence makes
That knows no joy, nor searching agony,
But like the calmness of a mill-pond, still,
Shallow, motionless and without use
Is dead.
Compare that stagnant pool to heaving ocean,
Now softly rippling, moon-kiss'd, in the night,
Or marching waves and spindrift mist
Beneath a lurid light.
So full of moods the sea, as one who loves,
With passion, fury, gentleness all one
To draw the wandering spirit to it's home.
Tis thus with love, but reason, never!

Fire Of Love

Consume thyself, O love
Burn thy flame bright
Seeming inexhaustible
To guttering candle.
This feeble frame
Cannot in peace endure,
But like an aging star
Bright with nuclear fire,
Or distant quasar
In the spatial night,
Glowing now
With ever brighter light,
Will fall upon itself
In final holocaust,
And be a dead cold world
That never can ignite.

Such ultimate
This humble heart
Can contemplate
With equanimity
Were it eternity.
But to exist
Without thy pain
O love, no spark
To light the everlasting dark
Within this spirit.
See inspiration
In thy lovely face
No more, nor hear
Thy softest sound,
Or ever know thy touch again,
But feel the salty rain
Of tears upon my cheek.

So thus I speak
To thee, O love,
Burn out thy fire,
Be thine own
Funeral pyre,
And leave this aching heart
To rest and heal this wound
In peace, lest one more cry
Should see it die.
And I alone
Alive within a tomb,
Or as a burnt-out stone
No love has known.

The Place I Know

There is a place I know,
Far leagues from here,
Where the bright roses grow
And life's fair stream runs clear.

There no grey shadow falls
Across bare sward,
But the bright birds recall
Sweet love's soft-spoken word.

Caprice

Imprisoned high within thy tallest tower
I see beneath me, bright with summer flowers
Thy meadows, girt with trees and sunlit bowers
Wherein thy favourites beguile the hours
Of day and night.
But I, a victim of thy light caprice,
Curs'd with thy pain that burns without surcease,
Have pleaded long the favour of release
From thy sweet bondage, but thy pangs increase.

Oh Love! Is there no let upon thy rack
Whereon my heart lies prostrate
Torn between thy fullness and thy lack.

Night Blue

I heard my voice cry
"I love you"
Awoke
And found myself
Beneath a radiant sky,
Night blue
And full of stars,
Wherein I sought your face.
But love,
That held my heart,
Then whispered
"Seek another place".
So turning,
Felt your hand in mine
And saw your eyes
Wide-open
And full of tears.
Your hair
Alight
With night's reflections,
Dark
Against the white
Linen and pale skin,

And love
Like a banner
With it's word
Printed on your mouth. I touched you
And the salt
Ran down your cheek.
Your smile
In greeting matched my own.
At once
Your beauty blazed about me.
The fire,
Soft and brilliant,
Took me by the throat.
Breathless
We kissed
And kissed again, and sighed
And slept.
When dreams
That would not be denied
Lay lightly
On me,
And I heard the voice that cried
"I love you".

The Sweet Sleep

Beauty is within the beholder's eye.
So say philosophers, but you and I,
Lock'd in love's night-long clasp,
Seek not to see,
Nor have we need to ask,
Where Beauty lies.

And when the moonlight dies
Beneath the paling skies
Of day,
Oblivious we lay,
And deep
In the sweet sleep
Of Passion.

Love's Caress

I stood as one afraid,
Or as a child might stand
Before the sea,
That feels the coursing shallows
On his feet,
Promising delights,
But fears the booming breakers.
In the night,
Awake
I felt your hands
Enclosing my frail heart,
And heard your voice,
Soft with love's caress,
Speak through the hiding dark
And say, "I fail you not."
I whispered, "True,
"I fear lest I fail you."

Dream Sweet

Sleep well, my darling
In the angels' care.
Sleep well,
Until the fair
Sweet wind of day-break
Lifts the nodding blooms
In brief caress,
And on the windows press
About your room.

Dream sweet, my darling
With a quiet mind.
Dream sweet,
Until the kind
Gray light of morning
Stirs the drowsing birds
To make their song.

Moonbeams

Come, take my hand
And let us walk
The glimmering moonbeams light
Across the shimmering sea.
While all around us
In the balmy night,
So faint and far beyond the sight
Of straining eyes,
The gentle monster lies
Asleep.

With rhythmic heaving
Of the breathing waves,
And every once again
A stir of dreams
To shake the pale moonbeams
And break in moment
The bewitching spell,
As now we wander
To the heart and well
Of all delight.

The Night

Sleep now.
Nor have I need of dreams,
For in thine arms
I have embraced the stars
And in thy face
Have glimpsed the gates
Of Paradise.

Oh! Ecstasy there lies
About thee, clothed
In scents of Spring,
By healing sun betrothed,
And in wide rivers bring
The joy of water,
Clear, cool and sparkling
Bright.

Sleep on, sweet night
And marry with the dawn,
That I may see thee
In the paling light
Ere thou tak'st flight
Before the sun.

When Morning Comes

Good-night, my love, good-night;
I'll not say you farewell,
For when the morning comes
In the bright misty spell
Of Spring, and the early stirring birds
Begin their first faint calls
Across the placid water,
And the soft dawn breeze
Stirs the nodding daffodils
To bring the scents of day,
Of dew-strewn meadows
And the budding trees,
As the darkness lifts
And night's spent shadows flee,
I'll wake, and hear your beating heart
Lie close to me.

Now You Are Gone

My footsteps trace
the scented paths
Held now in bond of memory
Long after you are gone,
And with each pace
I see you, face to face;
And in the lofty corridors and halls
Behind the blank locked doors
Your whispered, lilting voice
Still calls.

Oh, blessed time,
That carries sweet Nepenthe in your arms,
Whose warm breath clouds the mirror of the mind
To ease dark sorrow's pangs,
And lose among the drifting mists of age
The bright sharp images of long ago.
Withhold your touch
And cease the idle circle of the hours,
Be still,
And let the light of eager fires,
That burn forever in the generous heart,
Illuminate the solitary path
I walk.

Alone

In a garden full of lilies
Tall and pale, like trumpets blown,
By the Islands of the Scillies
Do I wander, now alone.

As the softly scented breezes
From the Western Ocean flow,
And my time takes out it's leases
In my patient to and fro.

'While I listen for the lost bells
Of the city 'neath the sea,
As I put my ear to sea-shells
Then I hear you speak to me.

From the farthest lands where ever
Shines the sun from clearing skies,
And the plumaged birds are never
Silent from their raucous cries.

Comes the voice that makes my heart ache
Calling through the mists of time,
Spanning all the years of waiting
Saying always "You are mine".

Waiting

How long and lonely are the waiting days
That hang upon the time, as idle thoughts
With endless repetition, all unsought,
For you, returning from the wand'ring ways.

Where I walk, head high in deepest forest,
Between the knotted columns of the trees
Full of dark assurance. Alone I rest,
Consoled by whispering voices in the breeze

There to confide my secret to the earth,
And with another eye, in distant lands,
I see your footsteps on the springing turf
Tracing the naked prints on foreign sands
Scorched beneath an ever-open sun
Or bathed in silky waters of the dawn.

Now, Love's brilliant rapier withdrawn
And from the starred wound dark drops appear
Upon a marble skin, like crimson tears
Or rubies from the mines of old Ceylon.
The thrust lies deep, straight to the pulsing heart
Transfix'd, that all reluctantly, to part
With life's warm blood,
Beats out its life.

The Return

I thought I heard soft voices calling
Across a clouded sea,
Where a vapourous dawn was paling
Calling you back to me.

I thought I saw the white birds flying
Above the wintered trees,
Beneath a sky where light was dying
Flying you back to me.

Love In Old Age

On summer days
I like to walk the dogs
Along the river-bank,
And sit on logs
Of long-dead trees;
To feel the breeze
Upon my face, and hear
The sussuration
And slow pace
Of water
Sliding over stones,
Smooth placed
By passing centuries.
Here I can rest
And watch the busy bustle
Of their play.
Here I reflect
Upon the days long past,
When love was ardent
Fleeting

Twixt passion and despair.
There was ecstasy
And agony,
Light and dark,
Hope and rejection,
Disillusion
Bitterness and pain.
Naught of that remains,
But,
Veiled by the passing of the years,
There is a certain beauty in those tears.

Now the flame burns true
And clear and bright
Constant as the Northern Star.
A light
Amid the gathering shadows,
A beacon
For the mansions of the night.

Grace

As I sit here, and let my wandering gaze
Rest on your hair, and part-averted face,
My aimless thoughts, adrift in secret space,
Take root, and in their conscious say, what grace
Is there, in that exquisite line,
No hand of man could form, nor mine
Describe
That beauty which you give, in sweet design.

The Leaving

If but a single memory remains
When I am gone,
Then let it count among the gains
Of love alone.

Or one word I have writ stay in your heart,
Let it relent
I pray you, do not let us part
Indifferent.

For if this love a single happy thought
To you has sent,
That is the happiness I sought
And am content.